Contents

Heat from the Earth

The word geothermal comes from the Greek words *ge* (meaning Earth) and *therme* (heat). Geothermal energy is produced by heat from the Earth.

This heat comes from deep inside our planet, and we can use its power to work machines, as well as to heat our homes, offices and factories. The term energy also comes from a Greek word, *energos*, which means active or working.

Energy sources help other things become active and do work, such as lifting or moving objects. For example, geothermal power can be used to make electricity. So when you switch on a light in your home, the energy to make it work might have come from the Earth's heat.

These people are enjoying the warm waters of a thermal pool on a volcanic island. The island is off the Antarctic Peninsula, near the South Pole, where the ocean is usually freezing.

ENERGY SOURCES
Facts · Issues · The Future

GEOTHERMAL POWER

NEIL MORRIS

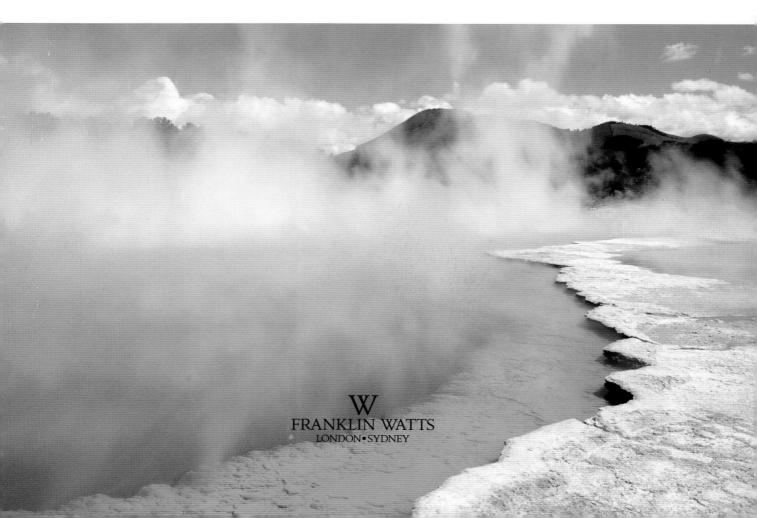

W
FRANKLIN WATTS
LONDON • SYDNEY

An Appleseed Editions book

First published in 2006 by Franklin Watts

Paperback edition 2008

Franklin Watts
338 Euston Road, London NW1 3BH

Franklin Watts Australia
Level 17/207 Kent St, Sydney, NSW 2000

© 2006 Appleseed Editions

Created by Appleseed Editions Ltd, Well House,
Friars Hill, Guestling, East Sussex TN35 4ET

Designed by Guy Callaby
Edited by Mary-Jane Wilkins
Artwork by Graham Rosewarne
Picture research by Su Alexander

ISBN 978 0 7496 7769 5

Dewey Classification: 333.8'8

A CIP catalogue for this book is available
from the British Library

Photographs by
Front cover: Bob Krist/Corbis; Title page Greg Probst/Corbis; 4 Kevin Schafer/
Corbis; 5 Alison Wright/Corbis; 7l Roger Ressmeyer/Corbis, r Bob Krist/
Corbis; 9t Bob Krist/Corbis, b Jim Sugar/Corbis; 10 Paul A. Souders/Corbis;
11t Paul A. Souders/Corbis, b Kevin R. Morris/Corbis; 12 James Leynse/Corbis;
13 Buddy Mays/Corbis; 14 Bettmann/Corbis; 15 Michael S. Yamashita/Corbis;
16 Mike McQueen/Corbis; 17 & 18 Roger Ressmeyer/Corbis; 21 Dave G.
Houser/Corbis; 22 Greg Probst/Corbis; 23t Roger Ressmeyer/Corbis,
b Mark Newham/Eye Ubiquitous/Corbis; 24 Jay Dickman/Corbis; 25 Bob
Krist/Corbis; 26-27 Michael S. Yamashita/Corbis; 27 (inset) Gary Braasch/
Corbis; 28 Richard T. Nowitz/Corbis; 29 David Ball/Corbis

Printed in China

Franklin Watts is a division
of Hachette Children's Books

Warm water

Much of the Earth's surface is covered by the water of the oceans. The surface temperature of the oceans varies from a warm 30°C near the equator to freezing near the North and South Poles. Just beneath the surface of the Earth, the water temperature also varies in different places. Inside a deep cave, the water might be very cold. But in places where underground water comes into contact with hot rocks, it heats up. This hot water can be used to generate geothermal power.

Natural steam power

We use many other energy sources – such as coal in a furnace or nuclear fuel in a reactor – to boil water. This makes steam, which in turn produces electricity (see page 19). But the Earth produces its own steam, so we don't need to burn anything else when we use geothermal energy. In areas of thermal pools and springs, steam often reaches the surface and swirls about like smoke. This is natural steam power.

RENEWABLE RESOURCE

Geothermal power is a renewable resource, because it can be used again and again and is not in danger of running out. Some other energy sources, such as coal and oil, are burned and used up to produce power. Water, solar, wind and biomass power are also renewable forms of energy.

Natural steam pours from this hillside in Bolivia.

Inside our planet

If we could travel to the centre of our planet, the temperature would go on rising throughout the journey. Beneath the Earth's crust, which forms its hard outer surface, is a much thicker layer called the mantle.

At the bottom of the crust the temperature is around 1000°C, and this increases by about one degree per kilometre as we go on down through the mantle. This layer is about 2,900 kilometres thick, and much of it is made up of molten rock. At the planet's centre is the core. This is made up of an outer layer of red-hot, molten iron and nickel, and a solid inner sphere. In the inner core the pressure is enormous and the temperature climbs to about 7000°C, which is hotter than the surface of the Sun! We are able to use just a tiny amount of this geothermal heat at the surface, where we live.

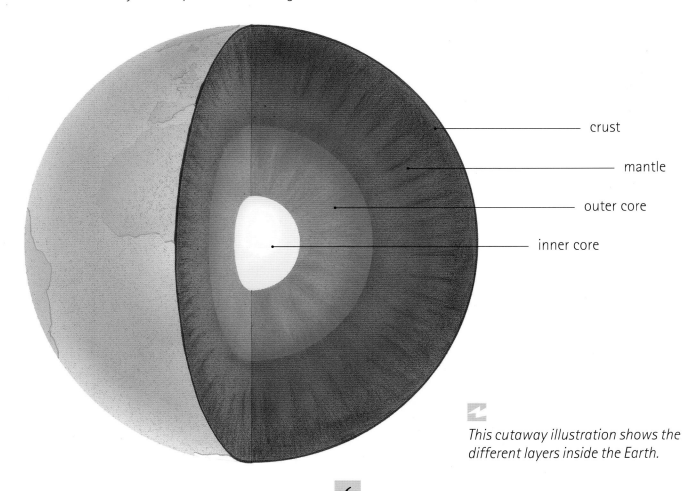

crust

mantle

outer core

inner core

This cutaway illustration shows the different layers inside the Earth.

Drilling down

The distance to the centre of the Earth is more than 6,000 kilometres. At the surface, the thickness of the crust varies from as little as five kilometres beneath the oceans up to more than 50 kilometres beneath the continents. Scientists have worked out what it is like inside the Earth by measuring the shock waves of earthquakes. The deepest anyone has ever drilled is just over 12 kilometres down. The borehole was made on the Kola Peninsula, in northern Russia. Engineers found that the temperature at the bottom of the hole was more than 200°C – twice as hot as boiling water.

Engineers use drilling rigs like this one to find the right spots for collecting geothermal energy. Some drill down to a depth of 3000 metres.

Geothermal oven

In some parts of the world, people traditionally use heat from the Earth for cooking. This custom may go back hundreds or even thousands of years. It shows how the Earth's heat can come right up to the surface. Near the town of Furnas, on one of the islands of the Azores in the Atlantic Ocean, locals make a traditional stew of meat and vegetables. To cook it, they simply lower their cooking pot into a hole in the ground.

These Azores islanders take their cooked stew from the ground.

Volcanic world

The Earth's crust is not made of one continuous layer, like an eggshell. It is cracked into huge pieces, called plates, which fit together like a giant jigsaw.

As heat from the mantle rises up into the crust, it makes the solid plates move very slowly – just a few centimetres each year. As the plates move, they rub against each other, and their squeezing and buckling can cause volcanoes. These are openings where molten rock, called magma, forces its way through cracks in the crust. The volcanic regions of the world are generally near the edge of plates, where one plate is forced beneath another. These areas are useful for geothermal power, because the Earth's heat comes right up to the surface.

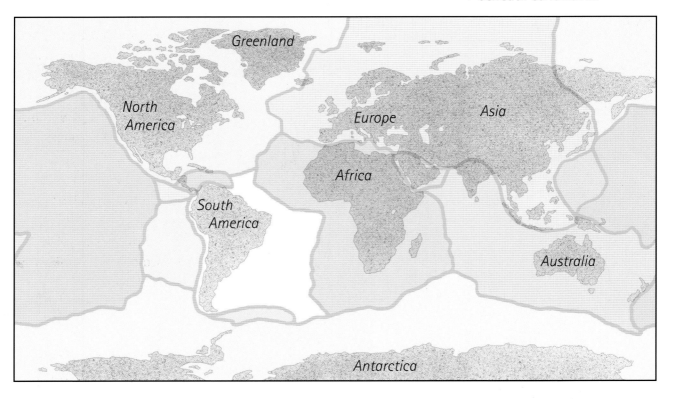

This map shows the boundaries of the world's major plates. Some boundaries are under oceans, and others beneath continents.

Greenland

North America

Europe

Asia

Africa

South America

Australia

Antarctica

Through the cracks

Some plates move apart beneath the ocean, leaving a crack where magma comes to the surface and forms new crust. This makes a ridge of underwater mountains, and sometimes peaks appear above the surface of the water and form islands. Both Iceland and the Azores lie on a long volcanic ridge in the middle of the Atlantic Ocean. When there is a volcanic eruption in Iceland, magma spurts through cracks. On the surface we call the molten rock lava.

Cracks run through Iceland as two plates very slowly move apart. This is a major area for geothermal power.

Hot spots

Other volcanic islands are formed as the ocean floor moves very slowly over a specially hot area beneath the Earth's crust. This is called a hot spot, and the Pacific islands of Hawaii were formed this way. The islands have many active volcanoes, including one called Kilauea that has been erupting continuously since 1983. This active volcanic area is used by the Hawaiians for geothermal power.

A fountain of lava spews out of Kilauea volcano, in Hawaii.

Hot springs and geysers

In areas where magma lies just below the surface of the Earth there are hot springs and thermal pools. Rainwater seeps underground through cracks and reaches rocks that have been heated up by the molten magma.

The hot, steaming water rises back up to the surface, where it may form a pool or just give off steam from rocks (as in the photograph on page 5). Some springs build up such a force that water and steam regularly shoot up though a hole or crack. We call these geysers, and the most explosive examples shoot water more than 100 metres into the air. Their name comes from the Great Geysir in Iceland, which was first mentioned many centuries ago and named after the Icelandic word for gusher.

This Icelandic geyser, called Strokkur (the churn), spouts for a few seconds every eight minutes.

Mud pots and fumaroles

Sometimes small amounts of water are heated underground. The steam may force its way to the surface through layers of volcanic ash and clay. As steam leaks through the surface layer, bubbling and plopping, it forms a mud pot. Steam and hot gases may also escape through small holes in firmer ground, forming fumaroles (or smokers). There are whole fields of mud pots and fumaroles in volcanic regions of Iceland, New Zealand and the United States.

Mineral terraces

Where a thermal pool forms on high ground, hot water flows downhill. The water is often filled with minerals that dissolved in it as it made its way to the surface. The minerals, such as chalk and lime, may build up over thousands of years to form flat layers, or terraces. Some of the most spectacular mineral terraces are in Yellowstone National Park, Wyoming, where there are more than 200 geysers and thousands of hot springs.

Mud pots steam and sputter in the Waiotapu thermal area of New Zealand. The area has been protected since 1931.

Minerva Terrace, at Mammoth Hot Springs in Yellowstone National Park, Wyoming.

BEAUTIFUL AND USEFUL?

Large amounts of geothermal energy are mainly available in volcanic regions. Many areas with hot springs and geysers are naturally beautiful and have become tourist attractions. Some are national parks. It is difficult to exploit geothermal energy without spoiling the look of the landscape. On the other hand, geothermal plants take up very little land compared with other power plants, because they sit right on top of their fuel source.

In ancient times

People probably started using thermal pools for bathing many thousands of years ago. The first people to use hot springs for bathing houses were the ancient Romans.

In the most northerly region of the Roman empire, at present-day Bath in the west of England, the Romans came across a warm spring. Historians believe this may have been used by Celtic Britons as a special place to worship Sulis, their goddess of healing. The Romans settled there and called it Aquae Sulis (Waters of Sulis).

Some time during the 1st century AD, Roman engineers built a lead-lined stone chamber around the sacred spring, which they dedicated to their own goddess, Minerva. They then built a large rectangular bath, like a modern swimming pool, which was fed with hot water directly from the spring.

The Roman bath at Bath used geothermal energy in the form of a hot spring.

Understanding the world

In the 5th century BC the Greek philosopher Empedocles taught that the world was made up of four elements – air, earth, fire and water. He said that everything else was made up of a combination of these elements. During the following century another Greek philosopher, Aristotle, said that there were underground fires in the Earth. He also thought that the Earth was riddled with caves that sucked in wind. When the fires lit the winds, they exploded and caused volcanoes and earthquakes.

Native Americans

There are many hot springs in North and South America, and most were used by ancient Native Americans thousands of years ago. The Tonopah springs in Arizona were named by people of the early Hohokam tribe, and the name means 'hot water under the bush'. The Native Americans used thermal areas as sacred healing places.

A peaceful creek in Hot Springs National Park, Arkansas. This area was a Native American homeland long before Europeans arrived in North America.

Developing industry

The Italians were the first to harness geothermal power for industry during the early 19th century. There is an area of hot springs and fumaroles west of the city of Siena in Tuscany. There Francesco Larderel (1789–1858) set up a plant to produce a chemical called boric acid.

At first he did this by burning wood to boil water from the springs, which contained a form of the mineral boron. Then, around 1830, he began to use the steam that came naturally out of the Earth instead. He even developed ways of using steam to drive pumps and drills.

In his honour, the thermal area was named Larderello and the mineral larderellite. The chemical works continued after Larderel's death, and in 1904 the area's geothermal steam was first used to produce electrical power. There is still a geothermal power station at Larderello today, as well as a museum dedicated to the founder of the industry.

This photograph from 1954 shows huge cooling towers beside the geothermal power plant at Larderello, Italy.

Town heating

During the 19th century American engineers also worked on ways of using geothermal steam. In 1892 a water company in Boise, the state capital of Idaho, amazed everyone by offering to supply houses with hot water as well as cold. To do this, the company used steam from hot springs near the town. The new district heating system was a great success, and is still used today.

Spa resorts

The Romans and others believed that the water and steam from geothermal springs were good for people's health. This was partly because of their warmth, and also because of the minerals contained in the water.

During the Middle Ages in Europe, some towns began to specialize in offering cures at their baths. Some of the most famous were Aachen and Baden-Baden in Germany. Another was the small town of Spa in Belgium, and this name – spa – was later given to any resort with mineral springs. During the 20th century many spas became even more important as health centres.

These steaming spa houses in Beppu, Japan, offer relaxing hot baths. Beppu lies in a region of hot springs.

Direct use

Almost all the homes and buildings in Iceland are heated by geothermal power. The people who first settled on the island around AD 870 called their settlement Reykjavik, meaning smoky bay.

But it was steam rather than smoke that they saw, rising from hot springs. Today, Reykjavik is the capital of Iceland, which is often called the land of ice and fire because icy glaciers lie next to hot springs and volcanoes. Icelanders have been using a geothermal system to heat their homes since 1928. There are hundreds of wells and thermal reservoirs in different areas of the island, and the water temperature rises to 350°C at 2000 metres below the ground. Geothermal hot water reaches home heating systems at about 80°C.

About 113,000 people live in Reykjavik. Most homes are heated by geothermal power.

Heating cycle

Five separate geothermal areas supply hot water for the Icelandic capital. The largest plant, at Nesjavellir, is 27 kilometres away from Reykjavik. There hot water from deep underground is used to heat cold water that is pumped in from nearby wells.

The geothermal hot water itself cannot be used because it contains so many minerals which would clog up the water pipes. The heated water is first pumped up through the mountains to a height of 400 metres, and from there it flows downhill to the city by gravity. The 80 cm-wide pipeline goes underground near Reykjavik. After circulating through the city, the water flows out through rainwater sewers. It is still warm, and is also used to melt ice on roads and pavements.

THE BLUE LAGOON

The Svartsengi power plant, in south-west Iceland, lies above a large geothermal reservoir. Most water seeps into the reservoir from the sea, so it is salty.

The plant has wells up to 2000 metres deep, and the boiling water heats nine towns as well as generating electricity. Some of the plant's waste water runs into a nearby lake, called the Blue Lagoon. Here people can bathe in water with an average temperature of 37°C. They believe the minerals in the water are good for the skin.

Bathers enjoy the warm water of the Blue Lagoon, beside Svartsengi power plant.

Generating electricity

Steam and hot water from underground are used to drive generators and produce electricity. The first-ever geothermal power plant, in Italy (see page 14), used steam only.

Some modern plants, such as those in the Geysers region of California, still work in a similar way. This is the largest known steam field in the world, and the first Geyser plant began generating electricity in 1960. Today, there are more than 350 steam wells and the plants there produce enough electricity to supply a city as big as San Francisco. The steam, which comes from up to four kilometres underground, is piped directly to turbines, where it turns blades that are linked to a generator.

This geothermal power plant lies near the town of Geyserville, in northern California. You can see steam from other plants in the distance.

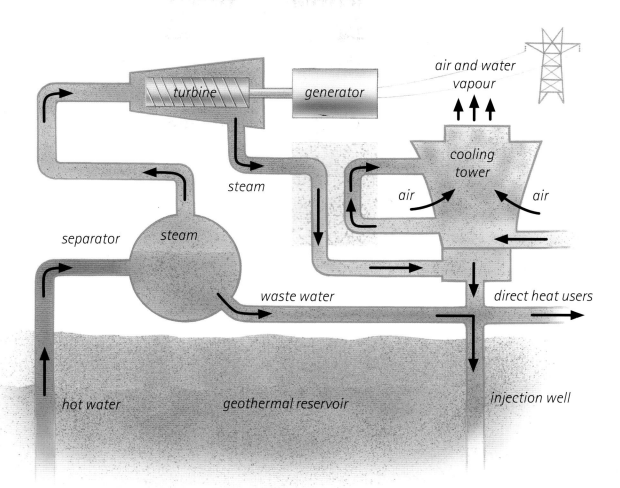

In the diagram:
turbine — generator — air and water vapour — cooling tower — steam — separator — steam — air — air — waste water — direct heat users — hot water — geothermal reservoir — injection well

Water and steam

When water is under pressure it boils at a higher temperature. This means that it can be hotter than 100°C underground and still be a liquid. For this reason, most geothermal regions produce very hot water rather than steam. In geothermal wells, the hot water rapidly vaporizes, or turns to steam, when it reaches the surface. The force of the steam is then used to turn a turbine. This is called a flash-steam plant, and it is the most common kind of geothermal power station.

Turbines and generators

Inside a power plant, turbines and generators change mechanical energy into electrical energy. The mechanical energy is the power of high-pressure steam, which turns the blades of a turbine connected by a shaft to a generator. Inside the generator, the shaft makes magnets spin inside wire coils to produce electricity. This technology was first used in 1831, when the British scientist Michael Faraday discovered that he could create electricity by moving a magnet through a coil of copper wire. The basic idea is still the same today and is used in all kinds of power stations.

This diagram shows how a flash-steam power plant works. The high-pressure water flashes to steam in a device called a separator. After passing through the turbine, the steam turns back to water and some returns to the underground reservoir. Some hot water is used for direct heating.

Heat pumps

The top few metres of the Earth's surface stay at a fairly constant temperature, in both summer and winter. This temperature is generally between 10°C and 16°C, and though this is warm rather than hot, it can help to heat buildings.

This is like a geothermal mini-system, which people can install in their homes. During the cold winter months, a geothermal heat pump uses underground heat to send warm air through a building. It can also be used to heat hot water. During the warm summer months, the system can work the other way, taking heat from the building and acting as a form of air conditioning.

heat pump

ground loop

How a geothermal heat pump system works in winter.

Simple system

A length of plastic pipe is laid in a loop beneath the ground outside the house, either flat (as shown in the diagram) or running straight down. An antifreeze solution is pumped through the pipe, which picks up the underground heat. The heat pump inside the house takes the heat from the solution and uses it to pump warm air through tubes throughout the building. This process is called heat exchange. The cool antifreeze solution then flows back through the underground loop to pick up more heat. If the house is too hot in summer, the system can be switched to work the other way round.

Many people swim in geothermally heated pools in Iceland. The pools often have steam and mud baths.

Heated pools

Iceland's geothermal system has been used to heat swimming pools for many years. Today, there are more than a hundred public pools on the island, and most are outdoors. In recent years, private owners have looked for ways to save on the cost of heating their pools. Geothermal heat pumps can be used for this purpose, as well as solar heating systems.

Around the world

The Earth's heat comes to the surface of all the world's continents, but it is much easier to use geothermal power in some regions than others.

At the beginning of the 21st century, the continent of North America produces most electricity from geothermal power, and the United States is the world's leading country. Next comes Asia, where the world's second-largest producer is the Philippines. Other large producers of geothermal electricity are Mexico, Italy and Indonesia, and other countries are also turning to the new technology.

The United States also makes most direct use of geothermal power (see pages 16–17), followed by the huge country of China and the very small one of Iceland. In 2005 planners in north-east England decided to build a new town on the site of an old mineral mine and supply 4000 homes with heating from hot rocks 800 metres underground.

New Zealand has many geothermal regions and a long history of using them for power. This is Champagne Pool, at Waiorapu, where the mineral-rich waters are 75°C.

These scientists are taking samples on volcanic Mount Pinatubo in the Philippines, on the Ring of Fire. The volcano last erupted in 1991.

The Olkaria power plant in Kenya.

Ring of Fire

The Ring of Fire is a roughly circular zone around the edges of the Pacific Ocean. It stretches for about 40,000 kilometres from New Zealand and east Asia to the coastlines of North and South America. Volcanoes, earthquakes and hot springs are common throughout the zone, caused by the Earth's plates crunching together (see page 8). Many of the world's biggest geothermal power producers lie on the Ring of Fire.

Great Rift Valley

The Great Rift Valley, in East Africa, is another region where the movement of plates causes geothermal activity. There is not much geothermal power production in Africa, but Kenya and Ethiopia – both on the Great Rift – are exceptions. The Olkaria power plant in Kenya has been in operation since 1981, and production started at the Ethiopian Aluto-Langano plant in 1999. Engineers in both countries expect to be using far more geothermal power by 2010.

Renewable benefits

Experts say there is no chance that geothermal power will lessen for thousands of millions of years. Much of the interior heat of the Earth comes from radioactive substances such as uranium in its crust and mantle.

These substances generate heat as they give off radioactivity, which we use as another form of power – nuclear energy. The constant production of heat deep inside the planet gives geothermal power an enormous advantage over non-renewable energy sources such as fossil fuels. Experts predict that reserves of coal will last little longer than 200 years, while oil and gas may run out in about 60 years time. Yet most of today's electricity is still produced by power stations burning fossil fuels.

This hot spring in Costa Rica is like a natural hot tub. The underground heat may one day disappear in this spot, but it will reappear somewhere else.

CLEAN AIR

The benefit of geothermal power and other renewable energy sources is that they do not pollute the atmosphere. Geothermal plants release a small amount of various gases, but they mostly give off excess steam, which eventually falls to Earth again as rain. This gives geothermal a great advantage over coal, oil and gas, which give off dangerous fumes when burned. Their exhaust gases include sulphur and nitrogen, as well as carbon dioxide, a greenhouse gas. This means that it stays high in the atmosphere, soaking up and trapping heat from the Sun.

Bananas grow in hot, damp climates – and in geothermal greenhouses in fairly cold Iceland.

Multipurpose resource

Geothermal energy has a wide range of uses, in addition to district heating and producing electricity. It is particularly useful for farmers and gardeners. Hot-water pipes provide under-soil heating for fields, as well as heat for greenhouses. This allows growers to cultivate vegetables and flowers out of season or in a cold climate. Many industrial processes need heat, and geothermal heat can be pumped direct to factories, as it is in Iceland.

Potential problems

Geothermal reservoirs often contain small amounts of various gases. These include hydrogen sulphide, which smells like rotten eggs. This can be removed at geothermal plants by devices called scrubbers.

ALTERING THE BALANCE

If hot water and steam are taken out of the ground through man-made boreholes and not replaced, a geothermal reservoir can be emptied and dried out. During the 1980s two active geysers in Nevada were destroyed by power plants when the water table was lowered. In the Rotorua region of New Zealand, too many boreholes were drilled and hot springs and geysers started to fail. Ten years after a special programme cemented up some holes and put waste water back underground, several extinct geysers started to gush again.

The reservoirs also contain carbon dioxide, which is released when water or steam come to the surface. But it amounts to less than one twenty-fifth of the carbon dioxide released by fossil fuels to produce the same amount of electricity. Underground thermal water also contains many minerals, which is why it was first used at Larderello (see page 14) and why it cannot be pumped directly through pipelines in Iceland. However, it is possible to separate the minerals and use them for other purposes.

Limited locations

One of the problems with geothermal power is that large amounts of underground energy are only easily available in certain parts of the world. These are generally volcanic regions, where areas with hot springs and geysers have become national parks. It is a challenge to exploit geothermal energy without spoiling the appearance of the landscape.

Local people protest against a geothermal plant in the Puna Forest of Hawaii. They feel it ruins the forest and that high levels of hydrogen sulphide make people ill.

Tourists enjoy a series of geysers and hot fields in the Rotorua region of New Zealand.

Future trends

Experts agree that renewable sources will become more and more important in future, as the world's demand for energy goes on increasing. According to forecasts, demand for electricity will nearly double over the next 25 years.

Today geothermal power forms a tiny percentage of total energy use, so the heat of the Earth is a vast resource that we scarcely use. However, the electricity it produces is expected to increase by at least a third in the next ten years. Direct use will increase even more, as scientists and engineers find new ways to distribute geothermal heat to communities and individual buildings. At the moment we are still dependent on fossil fuels, and in future we will all be encouraged to use our planet's energy more wisely and sparingly.

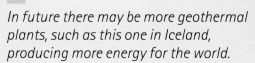

In future there may be more geothermal plants, such as this one in Iceland, producing more energy for the world.

Hot dry rock

For years scientists have been working on a geothermal technology known as hot dry rock (or HDR for short). The idea is to drill down to depths below 3 kilometres, where layers of rock are hot but there is no water. If water is sent down a deep borehole from the surface, it can make small cracks in the bed of hot rock. The water heats up and can be recovered though other boreholes and then used to drive a turbine and make electricity. Research projects in different parts of the world have shown that the HDR system works.

This diagram shows how the hot dry rock system works.

power plant

heat exchanger

cold water

hot water

Inside the parliament building in Germany's capital, Berlin. The building has its own geothermal system. In summer waste heat is pumped down to a natural water reservoir 300 metres below ground. Hot water is brought up to heat the building in winter.

NEW TECHNOLOGY

Future technology might help us develop geothermal power in new regions. In 2003 Germany opened its first geothermal power plant, following more than 20 other countries. There are also plans, in Munich and other German cities, to use geothermal power for district heating. Another way forward is to combine geothermal with other renewable sources, such as wind and solar power, so that we can better protect the environment.

Glossary

air conditioning A system for cooling the air in a building.

antifreeze solution A liquid that freezes at a lower temperature than water.

borehole A deep hole in the ground made by a drill.

continent One of the Earth's seven huge land masses.

cooling tower A tall structure in which used steam cools and turns back to water.

core The central part of the Earth.

crust The Earth's outer layer.

drilling rig A large framework that supports drilling equipment.

equator An imaginary line around the middle of the Earth.

fossil fuel A fuel (such as coal, oil and natural gas) that comes from the remains of prehistoric plants and animals.

fumarole A hole in the ground that releases geothermal steam and volcanic gases.

furnace An oven-like structure in which materials can be heated to very high temperatures.

generator A machine that turns mechanical energy into electrical energy.

geology The study of the structure of the Earth.

geothermal Produced by heat inside the Earth.

geyser A hot spring where boiling water and steam regularly shoot up high in the air.

glacier A slowly-moving river of ice.

greenhouse gas A gas, such as carbon dioxide, that traps heat from the Sun near the Earth and helps create a greenhouse effect.

hot spring A place where warm water comes from underground to form a pool on the surface.

lava Molten rock that pours out of a volcano.

magma Molten rock formed in the Earth's mantle.

mantle The thick layer of molten rock beneath the Earth's crust.

mineral A solid chemical substance that occurs naturally in the Earth.

molten Melted.

mud pot A place where geothermal steam bubbles through a surface layer of mud.

plate One of the large pieces of the Earth's crust.

pollute To damage with harmful substances.

power station A plant where electricity is generated.

radioactive Describing a substance such as uranium that gives off energy in the form of streams of particles.

radioactivity High-energy particles given off by radioactive substances.

reactor A device in which nuclear reactions are produced to release energy.

refinery An industrial plant where oil and gas are processed and purified.

safety valve A valve that opens automatically to release steam and reduce pressure.

scrubber A device that filters and cleans fumes as they pass through a chimney.

spa A mineral spring that is thought to be good for people's health; a resort with mineral springs.

thermal Of heat; also short for geothermal.

thermal (or geothermal) reservoir A natural underground store of hot water.

turbine A machine with rotating blades that turn a shaft.

Index